OPPOSITES

All Around Me!

NEW and

OLD

A Crabtree Roots Book

AMY CULLIFORD

CRABTREE
Publishing Company
www.crabtreebooks.com

T0020210

School-to-Home Support for Caregivers and Teachers

This book helps children grow by letting them practice reading. Here are a few guiding questions to help the reader with building his or her comprehension skills. Possible answers appear here in red.

Before Reading:
- What do I think this book is about?
  - *This book is about new things and old things.*
  - *This book is about the difference between old and new.*

- What do I want to learn about this topic?
  - *I want to learn the difference between old and new.*
  - *I want to learn what new things look like.*

During Reading:
- I wonder why...
  - *I wonder why trees can live to be so old.*
  - *I wonder why we keep old books.*

- What have I learned so far?
  - *I have learned that cars can be new or old.*
  - *I have learned what new trees look like.*

After Reading:
- What details did I learn about this topic?
  - *I have learned that trees grow taller the older they get.*
  - *I have learned that new and old are opposites.*

- Read the book again and look for the vocabulary words.
  - *I see the word **tree** on page 5 and the word **car** on page 8. The other vocabulary words are found on page 14.*

What is **new**, and what is **old**?

This **tree** is new.

This tree is old.

This **car** is new.

This car is old.

This **house** is new.

This house is old.

Word List

Sight Words

and   this

is   what

Words to Know

car   **house**   **new**

old   **tree**

31 Words

What is **new**, and what is **old**?

This **tree** is new.

This tree is old.

This **car** is new.

This car is old.

This **house** is new.

This house is old.

Written by: Amy Culliford

Designed by: Rhea Wallace

Series Development: James Earley

Proofreader: Ellen Rodger

Educational Consultant: Marie Lemke M.Ed.

Photographs:
Shutterstock: Chantanee: cover; Daboost: p. 1; Andy
Hoech: p. 3, 14; MagMac83: p. 4, 14; Serge Skiba:
p. 6-7; jamesteohart: p. 8, 14; Daniel Ocho: p. 9;
Breadmaker: p. 11, 14

All Around Me!

Library and Archives Canada Cataloguing in Publication

Title: New and old / Amy Culliford.
Names: Culliford, Amy, 1992- author.
  Description: Series statement: Opposites all around me! | "A Crabtree
  roots book".
Identifiers: Canadiana (print) 20210159375 | Canadiana (ebook)
  20210159383 | ISBN 9781427140203
  (hardcover) | ISBN 9781427140265 (softcover) | ISBN 9781427133595
  (HTML) | ISBN 9781427140326 (read-along ebook) | ISBN 9781427134196
  (EPUB)
Subjects: LCSH: Age—Juvenile literature. | LCSH: Polarity—Juvenile
  literature. | LCSH: English language—Synonyms and antonyms—Juvenile
  literature.
Classification: LCC PE1591 .C85 2021 | DDC j428.1—dc23

Library of Congress Cataloging-in-Publication Data

Names: Culliford, Amy, 1992- author.
Title: New and old / Amy Culliford.
Description: New York, NY : Crabtree Publishing Company, [2022] | Series:
  Opposites all around me - a Crabtree roots book | Includes index. |
  Audience: Ages 4-6 | Audience: Grades K-1
Identifiers: LCCN 2021010800 (print) | LCCN 2021010801 (ebook) | ISBN
  9781427140203 (hardcover) | ISBN 9781427140265 (paperback) | ISBN
  9781427133595 (ebook) | ISBN 9781427134196 (epub) | ISBN 9781427140326
  (read along)
Subjects: LCSH: New and old--Juvenile literature. | Polarity--Juvenile
  literature. | English language--Synonyms and antonyms--Juvenile
  literature.
Classification: LCC B105.N4 C85 2022 (print) | LCC B105.N4 (ebook) | DDC
  001--dc23
LC record available at https://lccn.loc.gov/2021010800
LC ebook record available at https://lccn.loc.gov/2021010801

Crabtree Publishing Company

www.crabtreebooks.com   1-800-387-7650

Copyright © 2022 **CRABTREE PUBLISHING COMPANY**   Printed in the U.S.A./062021/CG20210401

All rights reserved. No part of this publication may be reproduced, stored in a retrieval system or
be transmitted in any form or by any means, electronic, mechanical, photocopying, recording, or
otherwise, without the prior written permission of Crabtree Publishing Company. In Canada: We
acknowledge the financial support of the Government of Canada through the Canada Book Fund
for our publishing activities.

Published in the United States
Crabtree Publishing

347 Fifth Avenue, Suite 1402-145
New York, NY, 10016

Published in Canada
Crabtree Publishing

616 Welland Ave.
St. Catharines, Ontario L2M 5V6